JOHN MURPHY

IRISH SHOPFRONTS
and PUBS

W9-CLC-633

INTRODUCTION BY *Patrick O'Donovan*

CHRONICLE BOOKS
SAN FRANCISCO

First published in 1994 by
The Appletree Press Ltd
19–21 Alfred Street, Belfast BT2 8DL
Tel: +44 232 243074 Fax: +44 232 246756
Copyright © The Appletree Press Ltd, 1994
Printed in the EU. All rights reserved.

Irish Shopfronts and Pubs

First published in the United States in 1994
by Chronicle Books, 275 Fifth Street,
San Francisco, CA 94103

ISBN 0-8118-0413-5

9 8 7 6 5 4 3 2 1

Introduction

The village shop in Ireland with its small turnover, run by the Irish for the Irish, was originally a work place where there might be an enlarged window so that a cobbler or weaver could have better light for his work. Then when shops meant selling what other men made, there were furiously individual attempts to provide a façade that would attract a customer. When plate glass came to Ireland in the middle of the nineteenth century, the great sheets of glass tended to be divided up by pillars. Thus if a window got broken on a market day, not all of it went.

The result of this development and the influence of European styles of the time – classical, Gothic and art nouveau – was a brilliant explosion of domestic architecture so typically and recognizably Irish that it is rightly called vernacular. Why it should have happened is not so easy to explain. A shopkeeping class asserting itself against the Ascendancy? A love of colour hitherto repressed by poverty? An act of enchanting snobbery, or some vast, private national joke? An assertion of gentility, or a talent too long hidden by others in its native ground? On this we can do little more than speculate.

Perhaps the ultimate purpose of these pubs and shopfronts is the fascia or entablature that bears the name of the proprietor. All the small columns and glass rise to hold this horizontal board the whole length of the façade, and upon this the native imagination has run a small but gorgeous riot. Thus, above Irish pubs and shopfronts, you see names in a hundred different forms. There is cursive Victorian, art nouveau, classical, celtic revival, solid great capital letters, and there is vulgarity raised to an art form, with gold and carving and all the brash colours of a healthy spectrum.

All these are part of Ireland's unbroken tradition. They are unique, and will begin to be treasured when it is too late to save them. That happens everywhere with such objects. Yet these are not the crude by-products of some primitive or derivative art. They are part of a national culture that was denied its proper expression in other visual forms. Each one should be a joy to any observer.

Patrick O'Donovan

Pub, Belfast

Post Office, Dundrum, Co. Down

Pub, Ramelton, Co. Donegal

Pub, Ennistymon, Co. Clare

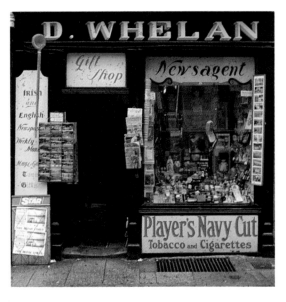

Newsagent & Tobacconist, Skibbereen, Co. Cork

Confectioner, Gort, Co. Galway

Pub-grocer, Ennistymon, Co. Clare

Hardware Store, Westport, Co. Mayo

Butcher, Sligo Town

General Store, Ahoghill, Co. Antrim

Pub, Cahir, Co. Tipperary

Pub, Corofin, Co. Clare

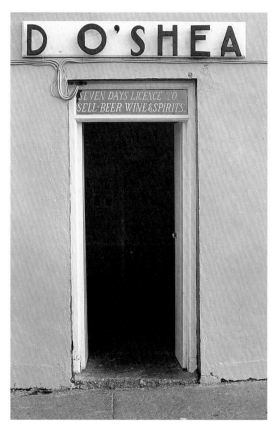

Pub, Sneem, Co. Kerry

General Store, Ennistymon, Co. Clare

Pub, Westport, Co. Mayo

Pub-grocer, Gort, Co. Galway

Pub, Ballycastle, Co. Antrim

Ironmonger & Grocer, Westport, Co. Mayo

Pub, Ennistymon, Co. Clare

Hardware Store, Ballycastle, Co. Antrim

Jeweller, Ennistymon, Co. Clare

Draper, Rosscarbery, Co. Cork

Hardware & Seeds, Gort, Co. Galway

Pub, Ennistymon, Co. Clare

Pub, Ennistymon, Co. Clare

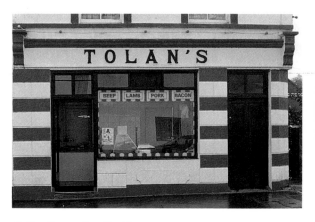

Butcher, Crossmolina, Co. Mayo

Butcher, Ballina, Co. Mayo

Pub, Westport, Co. Mayo

Pub, Westport, Co. Mayo

Pub, Lahinch, Co. Clare

Shoe Shop, Ballynahinch, Co. Down

Pub, Ennistymon, Co. Clare

Pub, Ennistymon, Co. Clare

Pub, Ballisodare, Co. Sligo

Provision Store, Gort, Co. Galway

Pub, Newport, Co. Mayo

Hardware Shop, Kilkeel, Co. Down

Drapers, Sligo Town

Outfitters, Newport, Co. Mayo

Saddler, Sports & Music Shop, Bantry, Co. Cork

Drapery, Kenmare, Co. Kerry

Auctioneers & Funeral Parlour, Kilkeel, Co. Down

Hardware Store, Ennistymon, Co. Clare

Hardware Store, Nenagh, Co. Tipperary

Grocer, Milltown Malbay, Co. Clare

Ironmongers & Furniture Shop, Listowel, Co. Kerry

Pub, The Neale, Co. Mayo

Pub, Ballymote, Co. Sligo

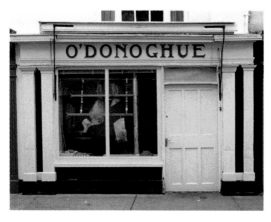

Butcher, Skibbereen, Co. Cork

Pub, Belfast

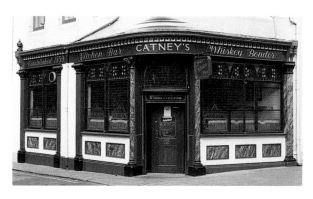

Pub, Belfast

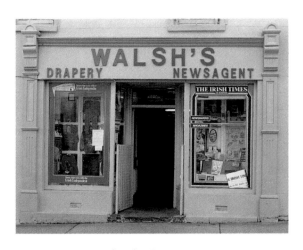

Draper & Newsagent, Ballinrobe, Co. Mayo

Bakery & General Store, Ennistymon, Co. Clare

Pub, Kilkenny Town

Pub, Dublin

Ennistymon, Co. Clare